PENGUIN BOOKS

IN THE WORDS OF NELSON MANDELA

Jennifer Crwys-Williams is a South African journalist and
broadcaster.

# In the Words of Nelson Mandela

*A Little Pocketbook*

Edited by Jennifer Crwys-Williams

PENGUIN BOOKS

PENGUIN BOOKS

Published by the Penguin Group
Penguin Books Ltd, 27 Wrights Lane, London W 8 5 T Z, England
Penguin Putnam Inc., 375 Hudson Street, New York, New York 10014, USA
Penguin Books Australia Ltd, Ringwood, Victoria, Australia
Penguin Books Canada Ltd, 10 Alcorn Avenue, Toronto, Ontario, Canada M 4 V 3 B 2
Penguin Books (NZ) Ltd, Private Bag 102902, NSMC, Auckland, New Zealand

Penguin Books Ltd, Registered Offices: Harmondsworth, Middlesex, England

First published by Michael Joseph 1998
Published in Penguin Books 1999
10 9 8 7 6 5 4 3 2 1

The editor and publisher would like to thank the following for permission to quote
from copyright material: Fatima Meer, *Higher Than Hope*, Penguin, 1990; Patti
Waldmeir, *Anatomy of a Miracle*, Viking, 1997

Set in Monotype Joanna
Printed and bound in Great Britain by
Butler & Tanner Ltd, Frome and London

This book is dedicated to the children of South Africa in the hope that as they grow they may find inspiration from the thoughts of Nelson Rolihlahla Mandela – and that, in his words on receiving the Nobel Peace Prize, they and other children the world over, may 'play in the open veld, no longer tortured by the pangs of hunger or ravaged by disease or threatened with the scourge of ignorance, molestation and abuse . . . Children are the greatest of our treasures.' In particular, it is for the children in my own family, living in both the old and the new worlds: Amber, Cassandra, Sebastian and Phoebe.

## Acknowledgements

Without the help of the marvellous Susan Segar, political correspondent of the *Natal Witness*, this book, quite literally, would not have been completed. It is rare to find a researcher who so completely understands what is needed that virtually everything that is wanted is used – as it was in this case.

Many thanks to Solly Masolo for helping me with research. My thanks too to Jill van Zyl and to the boffins who helped create (and run) the ANC home page (http://www.anc.org.za). As always, Nancy Ncube's generosity of spirit went beyond the normal confines of friendship.

My agent, Carole Blake of Blake Friedmann Ltd, and the staff of that company, have encouraged me with their enthusiasm. Rowland White of Michael Joseph has been a supportive and sensitive editor, and one with nerves of steel.

My special thanks to all the journalists who, over the years, have interviewed Nelson Mandela with skill and with passion, and who have provided me with much of the material used in this book. In particular, my thanks to the foreign correspondents, past and present, who helped me enormously.

# Introduction

It is the fate of very few human beings to transcend the limits of their national boundaries and to become the property of the world. As this turbulent century and the millennium in which it finds itself draw to an end, the shadow cast by the slight figure of India's Mahatma Gandhi has touched virtually every nation on earth, as has that of Martin Luther King, Jnr. Both fought for the freedom of their own oppressed people, and in doing so fought for the freedom and dignity of people in far-flung lands, for freedom, dignity and hunger know no national boundaries.

So, too, has the almost messianic figure of South Africa's Nelson Rolihlahla Mandela stretched out to capture the hearts and the imaginations of the world's teeming peoples. How ironic that two of these men – the Mahatma and Mandela – should have intimately known the soil of the beloved country, South Africa, and to have been affected by its sweeping beauty, its grandeur, its turbulent history and its racial prejudices in similar ways.

Was it just coincidence that all three men lit beacons which flamed across the world as they preached, sometimes with breathtaking courage and with a stubborn disregard for the personal consequences their message might bring, the credo of non-racialism? How ironic it was that Martin Luther King, Jnr's 'I Have a Dream' speech, which ended with: 'Free at last! Free at last! Thank God almighty, we are free at last!', should have been made as Nelson Mandela was one year into his twenty-seven years' incarceration – and that Nelson Mandela should have uttered those selfsame words in 1994 as he cast his vote in South Africa's first democratic election.

Known to his countrymen and women as Madiba, Nelson Mandela is the world's role model. A towering figure of strength and forgiveness, he has been able to do the almost impossible: unite the bitterly divided people of the country of his birth. In so doing, he has been taken to the heart of both the mighty and the dispossessed the world over.

Nelson Mandela, whilst remaining a South African to the last fibre of his being, belongs to everyone, irrespective of where they live and, importantly for him, how they live. He has become, in the few years since his release from imprisonment, a symbol of reconciliation and, in a world divided by sectarian hatreds, a symbol of love.

He would protest: he avers that he is no saint – but to South Africans, Nelson Mandela's rainbow people, he has, quite simply, no parallel.

And perhaps his thoughts, reproduced on these pages, and honed over many years of tribulation and anguish, will inspire people, young and old, moneyed and impoverished, the world over. In particular, I hope it will inspire people who have had few role models in their lives, who have suffered their own apartheids in their own countries: there is light, there is hope and, above all, there is reconciliation.

Jennifer Crwys-Williams

## On Abortion

Women have the right to decide what they want to do with their bodies.

## On His Achievements

Don't tempt me to beat my chest and to say this is what I have done!

I must not be isolated from the collective who are responsible for the success.

I make a mistake, I normally say: 'It's these ...... chaps,' and when they do something good, I say: 'This is the man.'

To illustrate his point, Madiba beat his chest – this was in an internationally televised interview, December 1997: Mandela Meets the Media.

## On Africa

For centuries, an ancient continent has bled from many gaping sword wounds.

No doubt Africa's renaissance is at hand – and our challenge is to steer the continent through the tide of history.

The people of the continent are eager and willing to be among the very best in all areas of endeavour.

The peoples of resurgent Africa are perfectly capable of deciding upon their own future form of government and discovering and themselves dealing with any dangers which might arise.

We need to exert ourselves that much more, and break out of the vicious cycle of dependence imposed on us by the financially powerful: those in command of immense market power and those who dare to fashion the world in their own image.

It would be a cruel irony of history if Africa's actions to regenerate the continent were to unleash a new scramble for Africa which, like that of the nineteenth century, plundered the continent's wealth and left it once more the poorer.

Conflict threatens not only the gains we have made but also our collective future.

frican rebirth is now more than an idea –
its seeds are being sown in the regional
communities we are busy building and in the
continent as a whole.

Can we continue to tolerate our ancestors being
shown as people locked in time?

Africa yearns and deserves to redeem her glory,
to reassert her centuries-old contribution to
economics, politics, culture and the arts, and
once more to be a pioneer in the many fields of
human endeavour.

One destabilizing conflict anywhere on the
continent is one too many.

A continent which, while it led in the very
evolution of human life and was a leading centre
of learning, technology and the arts in ancient
times, has experienced various traumatic epochs,
each one of which has pushed her peoples deeper
into poverty and backwardness.

# On Being an African

Teach the children that Africans are not one iota inferior to Europeans.

*From his seminal 'No Easy Walk to Freedom' speech, 21 August 1953.*

The lack of human dignity experienced by Africans is the direct result of the policy of white supremacy.

*Spoken from the dock at the Rivonia Treason Trial, 20 April 1964, which sent him to prison for twenty-seven long years.*

All of us, descendants of Africa, know only too well that racism demeans the victims and dehumanizes its perpetrators.

We are rising from the ashes of war.

*He said this while presenting the Africa Peace Award to the war-torn country of Mozambique in November 1997. Madiba's companion, Graça Machel, is the widow of the former president of that country and he feels a great bond with it.*

# On the African National Congress

As no man is an island, so too are we not men of stone who are unmoved by the noble passions of love, friendship and human compassion.

*He was referring to the formation of the ANC Youth League on Easter Sunday, . Mandela and his lifelong friends Oliver Tambo and Walter Sisulu were prominent among its founding fathers — the young Turks of their day. This quotation was from a speech made in Uppsala Cathedral, Sweden, in March 1990.*

We must move from the position of a resistance movement to one of builders.

For us the struggle against racism has assumed the proportions of a crusade.

The African nationalism for which the ANC stands is the concept of freedom and fulfilment for the African people in their own land.

Human rights and the attainment of justice have explicitly been at the centre of our concerns.

I have always been a member of the African
National Congress and I will remain a member of
the African National Congress until the day I die.


## On *Afrikaners*


As those who drew benefits from a previous
programme of affirmative action, they should
realize better than anyone else how such a
programme can contribute towards making the
community more productive.


I have often noticed Afrikaans people remark that
the new South Africa gives them a feeling of
freedom now that they have entered a wider
world of relationships with fellow South
Africans.

llenge of the New Patriotism is not one of
between Afrikanerdom and being South
African. On the contrary, it is precisely about the
healing reconciliation of Afrikaners with being
fully South African.

Maybe it was out of fear that they themselves
would one day become the oppressed once again.

On possible reasons for the Afrikaners oppressing fellow South Africans during
apartheid, and spoken in the tense run-up to South Africa's first democratic election in
1994.

When an Afrikaner changes, he changes
completely.

Many Afrikaners, who once acted with great
cruelty and insensitivity towards the majority in
our country, to an extent you have to go to jail to
understand, have changed completely and
become loyal South Africans in whom one can
trust.

## On Age

What nature has decreed should not generate undue insecurity.

I am nearing my end. I want to be able to sleep until eternity with a broad smile on my face, knowing that the youth, opinion-makers and everybody is stretched across the divide, trying to unite the nation.

*From a speech to students at the University of Potchefstroom, February 1996. He was seventy-seven; Nelson Mandela was born in the tiny Transkei village of Mvezo on 18 July 1918.*

I will be eighty-one when I finally retire, and I never thought a man in his seventies should take over an organization like the ANC.

## On Alliances

No true alliance can be built on the shifting sands of evasions, illusions and opportunism.

## On Anger

Anger is a temporary feeling — you soon forget it, particularly if you are involved in positive activities and attitudes.

It is not easy to remain bitter if one is busy with constructive things.

## On Apartheid

Apartheid is the rule of the gun and the hangman.

Apartheid itself was a war against the people.

The universal struggle against apartheid was not an act of charity arising out of pity for our people, but an affirmation of our common humanity.

Out of the experience of an extraordinary human disaster that lasted too long, must be born a society of which all humanity will be proud.

*At his inauguration as President of South Africa, 10 May 1994.*

It would have been immoral to keep quiet while a racist tyranny sought to reduce an entire people into a status worse than that of beasts of the forest.

The millions of graves strewn across Europe which are the result of the tyranny of Nazism, the decimation of the native peoples of the Americas and Australia, the destructive trail of the apartheid regime against humanity – all these are like a haunting question that floats in the wind: why did we allow these to happen?

Apartheid continues to live with us in the leaking roofs and corrugated walls of shacks; in the bulging stomachs of hungry children; in the darkness of homes without electricity; and in the heavy pails of dirty water that rural women carry for long distances to cook and to quench their thirst.

*He said this in November 1997, one month before stepping down as president of the ANC.*

At each turn of history, apartheid was bound to spawn resistance; it was destined to bring to life the forces that would guarantee its death.

## On a Bill of Rights

A Bill of Rights is an important statement about the nature of power relations in any society.

*The ANC has had a Bill of Rights since 1923.*

A Bill of Rights cannot be associated with the political or economic subordination of either the majority or the minority.

A Bill of Rights is a living thing.

## On Black Consciousness

Black consciousness has fired the determination of leaders and the masses alike.

The driving thrust of black consciousness was to forge pride and unity amongst all the oppressed, to foil the strategy of divide and rule, to engender pride among the mass of our people and confidence in their ability to throw off their oppression.

Above all, the liberation movement asserted that the people would most readily develop consciousness of their proud being, of their equality with everyone else, of their capacity to make history.

that black consciousness placed on
verberated across our land; in our
nd amongst the communities in exile –
and our people, who were once enjoined to look
to Europe and America for creative sustenance,
turned their eyes to Africa.

## On South African Blacks

The blacks think this transformation was brought
about by military victory, and they have defeated
the whites. They think the whites are lying on
the floor and begging for mercy.

From an interview during his July 1996 state visit to Britain.

## On Bosnia

They [the leaders] thought through their blood
and not through their brains.

## On Boxing

Any boxer with skill I admired.

I did not enjoy the violence of boxing as much as the science of it.

## On the British

I regard the British parliament as the most democratic institution in the world, and the independence and impartiality of its judiciary never fail to arouse my admiration.

Africa's greatest city.


## On Cape Town


It was here, three centuries ago, that sailors from
Europe triggered off the chain of the
dispossession whose consequences we are still
grappling with today.


In Cape Town resides part of the souls of many
nations and cultures, priceless threads in the rich
diversity of our African nation.


The city hosted me and my colleagues for over
twenty-six years.

*Robben Island lies off the coast from Cape Town and can be clearly seen from Table
Mountain. Cape Town, of course, was also the city which welcomed him on his first
day of freedom.*

## On Change

Belief in the possibility of change and renewal is perhaps one of the defining characteristics of politics and of religions.

## On Charity

Cash handouts might sustain you for a few months, at the end of which your problems remain.

## On His Childhood

When I was a boy brought up in my village in the Transkei, I listened to the elders of the tribe telling stories about the good old days, before the arrival of the white man.

In his autobiography, Long Walk to Freedom, Mandela writes touchingly about his childhood. His collaborator on the book was Time contributor Richard Stengel; it took eighteen months to write, starting with a manuscript Mandela had begun secretly in his prison cell. They began work daily at 6.45 a.m. – Mandela is an early riser to this day.

I hoped and vowed then that, among the treasures that life might offer me, would be the opportunity to serve my people and make my own humble contribution to the freedom struggle.

The elders would tell us about the liberation and how it was fought by our ancestors in defence of our country, as well as the acts of valour performed by generals and soldiers during those epic days.

## On Children

Children are the most vulnerable citizens in any
society and the greatest of our treasures.
Nobel Peace Prize ceremony, Oslo, Norway 1993.

The children must, at last, play in the open veld,
no longer tortured by the pangs of hunger or
ravaged by disease or threatened with the scourge
of ignorance, molestation and abuse, and no
longer required to engage in deeds whose gravity
exceeds the demands of their tender years.

The reward of the ending of apartheid will and
must be measured by the happiness and welfare
of the children.

The children who sleep in the streets, reduced to
begging to make a living, are testimony to an
unfinished job.

There can be no keener revelation of a society's soul than the way in which it treats its children.

Taken from his summary of the first year of the Nelson Mandela Children's Fund, 1996 (on the Worldwide Web at http://www.web.co.za/mandela/children).

## On Christmas

Christmas was the only time we children could have sugar and tea, and we were also given some syrup and bread and a sheep was slaughtered.

In prison they allowed us to buy a packet of sweets or a packet of fruit.

## On Circumcision

The pain went into the marrow of my bones.

I was not as forthright and strong as the other boys that preceded me.

The fact that courage is expected of you in the face of the unbearable gives you strength for the rest of your life.

## On Clothes

My father gave me his riding breeches and he cut them, and they had twine which I used as a belt, and that is how I went to school for the first time.

*He was describing his early Transkei childhood.*

I had a pair of shorts, sandals but no socks, a sleeveless shirt and no underwear, which is very humiliating.

*Talking to the then editor of French Vogue, December 1993, and referring to the early days of his imprisonment — a far cry from the 'Madiba style' shirts he has made famous. They are generally made of silk and lined with silk — and the pattern is perfectly aligned, making them costly in terms of fabric to make.*

There isn't a single article I wear that I have bought — people just generously give me clothes.

*After seven months as President, in 1994.*

Every time I put on a bow tie I am so
uncomfortable I can hardly talk.

Everybody just looks at my face – not at my clothes.

## On Colonialism

Through force, fraud and violence, the people of
North, East, West, Central and Southern Africa were
relieved of their political and economic power
and forced to pay allegiance to foreign monarchs.

The resistance of the black man to white colonial
intrusion was crushed by the gun.

Taken from Mandela's letter, smuggled out of Robben Island after the 1976 Soweto
uprising, and published internationally by the ANC in 1980.

## On Communication

One of our strongest weapons is dialogue.

## On Communism

For many decades communists were the only
political group in South Africa who were
prepared to treat Africans as human beings and
their equals; who were prepared to eat with us;
talk with us, live with us and work with us.

Spoken from the dock at the Rivonia Treason Trial, 20 April 1964.


There is so much hypocrisy behind some of this
red-baiting that it sickens me, and I feel like
saying to the culprits: 'How dare you say to me,
a man of seventy-five, that I must denounce my
friends, and for whom?'


## On Compromise

That is the nature of compromising: you can
compromise on fundamental issues.

At one of his first interviews after his release from twenty-seven years' imprisonment,
15 February 1990. He was released on 11 February 1990.

If you are not prepared to compromise, then you must not enter into, or think about, the process of negotiation at all.

Compromise must not undermine your own position.

Insignificant things, peripheral issues, don't need any compromise.

## On Conciliation

No organization whose interests are identical with those of the toiling masses will advocate conciliation to win its demands.

## On Conscience

Men must follow the dictates of their conscience
irrespective of the consequences which might
overtake them for it.

## On the South African Constitution

We give life to our nation's prayer for freedom
regained and a continent reborn.

On signing the new South African constitution into law at Sharpeville, 10 December
1996.

Let us now, drawing strength from the unity
which we have forged, together grasp the
opportunities and realize the vision enshrined in
this constitution.

Respect for human life, liberty and well-being
must be enshrined as rights beyond the power of
any force to diminish.

What challenges us is to ensure that none should enjoy lesser rights; and none tormented because they are born different, hold contrary political views, or pray to God in a different manner.

The key to the protection of any minority is to put core civil and political rights beyond the reach of temporary majorities by guaranteeing them as fundamental human rights, enshrined in a democratic constitution.

## On Criticism

If the criticism is valid, it must be made.

## On Culture

Like truth, culture and creativity are enduring.

## On His Culture

In my culture we don't discuss personal
questions with young people.

Our families are far larger than those of whites
and it is always a pleasure to be fully accepted
throughout a village, district, or even several
districts, accompanied by your clan, and be a
beloved household member, where you can call
at any time, completely relaxed, sleep at ease and
freely take part in the discussion of all problems,
where you can even be given livestock and land
to build, free of charge.

From an undated letter, written from Robben Island, to his cousin Sisi.

**Dead**

In eulogies to the departed, the works of the living sometimes bear little relation to reality.

The names of only very few people are remembered beyond their lives.

## On His Death

It would be very egotistical of me to say how I would like to be remembered. I'd leave that entirely to South Africans.

I would just like a simple stone on which is written, 'Mandela'.

Taken from a moving article for The New York Times Magazine by Anthony Lewis, 23 March 1997.

There will be life after Mandela.

## On Democracy

What is important is not only to attain victory for democracy, it is to retain democracy.


Democracy and human rights are inseparable.


A democratic political order must be based on the majority principle, especially in a country where the vast majority have been systematically denied their rights.


Even tyrants must be allowed to campaign.


Majority rule is not intended to suppress the views, the hopes, the aspirations, of the minority.

## On Demonstrations

Mass action is a peaceful form of channelling the anger of the people.

## On Determination

As long as you have an iron will you can turn misfortune into advantage.

From a letter to his daughter Zindzi, September 1990.

## On Discipline

Discipline is the most powerful weapon to get liberation.

An organization can only carry out its mandate if there is discipline, and where there is no discipline there can be no real progress.

## On Domesticity

I make my own bed every day. I don't allow the ladies who look after me to do it. I can cook a decent meal . . . I can polish a floor.

## On Education

Parents have the right to choose the kind of education that shall be given to their children.

Make every home, every shack or rickety structure a centre of learning.

# On Election Day (27–28 April 1994)

It was as though we were a nation reborn.

*Nelson Mandela was seventy-four when he cast his first vote.*

We can loudly proclaim from the rooftops: Free at last! Free at last!

*After Martin Luther King, Jnr (the closing words from his 'I Have a Dream' speech, Washington, DC, 28 August 1963). Nelson Mandela spoke the words on the first day of the first democratic South African election, 28 April 1994.*

I stand before you humbled by your courage with a heart full of love for all of you.

# On Emigration

To this day we continue to lose some of the best among ourselves because the lights in the developed world shine brighter.

# On Enemies

If a man fights back he is likely to get more respect than he would if he capitulated.

*At his Bishopscourt, Cape Town, press conference on 15 February 1990, his first after his release from twenty-seven years' imprisonment.*

I wanted South Africa to see that I loved even my enemies while I hated the system that turned us against one another.

*Mandela's presidency has been notable for the efforts towards reconciliation he has made – including taking tea in the all-white Boer enclave of Oranje with the widow of the architect of apartheid, Dr Hendrik Verwoerd, and meeting Dr Percy Yutar, prosecuting attorney at the Rivonia Treason Trial.*

Sitting down and denying the enemy the opportunity to use violence is the best strategy.

## On His Family

I have had to separate myself from my dear wife
and children, from my mother and sisters, to live
as an outlaw in my own land.

When your life is the struggle, as mine was,
there is little room left for family.

I rued the pain I had often caused my family
through my absence.

I did not in the beginning choose to place my
people above my family, but in attempting to
serve my people, I found I was prevented from
fulfilling my obligations as a son, a brother, a
father and a husband.

He has said this frequently, and might have added 'and as a grandfather'. In 1997 he
had twenty-one grandchildren.

Our political activities have just destroyed our family.

*Spoken after two and a half years as President of South Africa and referring, sadly, to his retirement, which he expects to be spent largely as a global statesman.*

One of my greatest pleasures is to sit down with my children and listen to them, to listen to their hopes and aspirations and helping them to grow.

To see your family, your children being persecuted when you are absolutely helpless in jail, that is one of the most bitter experiences, most painful experiences, I have had.

## On Favourite Things

My favourite animal is the impala because it is alert, curious, rapid and able to get out of difficult conditions easily – and with grace.

*Taken from French Vogue December 1993/January 1994. It was a historic issue – edited by Nelson Mandela himself – and now a collectors' item.*

Koeksusters are my favourite: in 1941 I was paid £2 a month and I reserved 10/- each weekend for koeksusters.

*Koeksusters are a sticky Afrikaans sweet: plaited dough, deep fried and dunked in cold syrup.*

My favourite pastime: reading.

## On Freedom

There is no easy walk to freedom.

*He was thirty-five when he made that statement in his famous 'No Easy Walk to Freedom' speech. The words were originally spoken by India's first prime minister after independence, Jawaharlal Nehru.*

Too many have suffered for the love of freedom.

*Still imprisoned, this was from his first speech in almost twenty-five years. It was read in Johannesburg to wildly cheering crowds by his youngest daughter, Zindzi, on 10 February 1985.*

No power on earth can stop an oppressed people determined to win their freedom.

*From 'The Struggle is My Life' press statement, 26 June 1961.*

There is no such thing as part freedom.

Only through hardship, sacrifice and militant action can freedom be won.

To men, freedom in their own land is the pinnacle of their ambitions, from which nothing can turn men of conviction aside.

We do not want freedom without bread, nor do we want bread without freedom.

Freedom is not only the opportunity to vote, but the gate to the awareness of many problems: hunger, poverty, illness, non-advancement.

To overthrow oppression is the highest aspiration of every free man.

*From Mandela's 'Black Man in a White Court' statement at his trial held in the Old Synagogue, Pretoria, from 15 October 1962 to 7 November 1962.*

A man who takes away another man's freedom is a prisoner of hatred.

*After twenty-seven years' imprisonment, Nelson Mandela walked to freedom through the gates of Victor Verster Prison, Paarl, at 4.16 p.m. on 11 February 1990.*

To be free is not merely to cast off one's chains, but to live in a way that respects and enhances the lives of others.

## On the Freedom Charter (1955)

The Freedom Charter is a political programme born of our struggle and rooted in South African realities.

It has received international acclaim as an outstanding human rights document.

The Charter is more than a mere list of demands for democratic reforms.

## On Friendship

Friendship and support from friends is something which is a source of tremendous inspiration always and to everyone.

Those who are ready to join hands can overcome the greatest challenges.

## On Government

When a government seeks to suppress a peaceful demonstration of an unarmed people by mobilizing the entire reserves of the state, military and police, it concedes powerful mass support for such a demonstration.

*Said in 1961, when he was living in hiding, and was referred to as the Black Pimpernel in the nation's press. A small monument has now been erected close to the spot where he was finally arrested on the night of 5 July 1962 outside the small KwaZulu/Natal town of Howick.*

That the will of the people is the basis of the authority of government is a principle universally acknowledged as sacred throughout the civilized world, and constitutes the basic foundations of freedom and justice.

Even when a democratic government is installed, no minority group should be disadvantaged.

There is always a danger that when there is no opposition, the governing party can become too arrogant – too confident of itself.

Government violence can do only one thing, and that is breed counter violence.

## On Government Corruption

Corruption in government – that is a plague that must be erased from every regime in every place in the world.

## On Harlem, New York City

Harlem symbolizes the strength and beauty in resistance and you have taught us that out of resistance to injustice comes renaissance, renewal and rebirth.

## On Health

The wounds that cannot be seen are more painful than those that can be treated by a doctor.

## On Heroes

No single individual can assume the role of hero or Messiah.

There are men and women chosen to bring happiness into the hearts of people – those are the real heroes.

## On His Heroes

Muhammad Ali was an inspiration to me even in prison because I thought of his courage and commitment. He used mind and body in unison and achieved success.

Kobie Coetsee – I have immense respect for that man because when no member of the National Party wanted to hear about the ANC, he was working systematically with me. He is one of my heroes.

Kobie Coetsee was Minister of Justice under P.W. Botha.

## On Himself

I have always regarded myself, in the first place, as an African patriot.

From the dock at the Rivonia Treason Trial, 20 April 1964. It took him two weeks, working in his cell at night, to write the speech.

I am a product of the mire that our society was.

I don't think there is much history can say about me.

I wanted to be able to stand and fight with my people and to share the hazards of war with them.

From the Rivonia Treason Trial, 20 April 1964.

I was made, by the law, a criminal, not because of what I had done, but because of what I stood for, because of what I thought, because of my conscience.

*Spoken at the Old Synagogue Trial, Pretoria, 7 November 1962.*

I am not a prophet and I am not in a position to say what we hope and desire in our lifetime.

I saw my mission as one of preaching reconciliation, of binding the wounds of the country, of engendering trust and confidence.

I felt fear more times than I can remember, but I hid it behind a mask of boldness.

I'm an ordinary person, I have made serious mistakes, I have serious weaknesses.

I will pass through this world but once, and I do not want to divert my attention from my task, which is to unite the nation.

*Spoken in February 1996, when he was seventy-seven years old.*

Sometimes I feel like one who is on the sidelines, who has missed life itself.

Rather than being an asset, I'm more of a decoration.

*Referring to himself as President of South Africa.*

People expect me to do more than is humanly possible.

I carry with me the frailties of my age and the fetters of prejudice that are a privilege of my years.

*He said this in 1997 in front of the International Olympic Committee, Lausanne, in a bid to persuade them to bring the Olympics to Cape Town in 2004.*

I seem to arrive more firmly at the conclusion that my own life struggle has had meaning only because, dimly and perhaps incoherently, it has sought to achieve the supreme objective of ensuring that each, without regard to race, colour, gender or social status, could have the possibility to reach for the skies.

## On History

History punishes those who resort to force and fraud to suppress the claims and legitimate aspirations of the majority of the country's citizens.

History shows that penalties do not deter men when their conscience is aroused.

Blaming things on the past does not make them better.

The past is a rich resource on which we can draw in order to make decisions for the future.

The purpose of studying history is not to deride human action, nor to weep over it or to hate it, but to understand it – and then to learn from it as we contemplate our future.

It is the dictate of history to bring to the fore the kind of leaders who seize the moment, who cohere the wishes and aspirations of the oppressed.

*He could have been speaking about himself; he was, in fact, speaking about the murdered black consciousness leader, Steve Bantu Biko, on the commemoration of the twentieth anniversary of his death (1997).*

More often than not, an epoch creates and nurtures the individuals which are associated with its twists and turns.

## On Home

I long to see the little stones on which I played as a child, the little rivers where I swam.

*Spoken with longing just after his release in 1990. When Nelson Mandela built his house in the village of Qunu, Transkei, where he was brought up, he built the house identically to the one he had lived in at Victor Verster Prison, Paarl. He says he 'became friendly with the walls of the house'. To this day, he says he was happiest there, between the years 1988 and 1990.*

Everybody comes back to where they were born.

*He was spending Christmas 1996 at Qunu. But for the years of his imprisonment, it was the modest Sowetan house he shared with his former wife, Winnie – No. 8115, Orlando West – which he dreamt about. In May 1997, together with his partner Graça Machel, he bought a new home in Houghton, Johannesburg, specifically to make space for his twenty-one grandchildren, some of whom live with him for extended periods.*

## On Homosexuality

There was a time when I reacted with revulsion against the whole system of being gay.

I was ashamed of my initial views, coming from a society which did not know this type of thing.

I understand their position, and I think they are entitled to carry on with what pleases them.

## On Honour

Which man of honour will desert a lifelong friend at the insistence of a common opponent and still retain a measure of credibility with his people?

From an open letter to P.W. Botha, State President of South Africa, March 1989, who had offered him a conditional freedom.

## On Housing

A man is not a man until he has a house of his own.

The families who live in shacks with no running water, sanitation and electricity are a reminder that the past continues to haunt the present.

## On Humanity

It is what we make out of what we have, not what we are given, that separates one person from another.

It is a fact of the human condition that each shall, like a meteor – a mere brief passing moment in time and space – flit across the human stage and pass out of existence.

From his address to the Joint Session of the Houses of Congress of the USA, Washington, DC, 26 June 1990, where he was rapturously received only months after his release.

To deny any person their human rights is to challenge their very humanity.

We fought injustice to preserve our own humanity.

Referring to the Robben Island years.

Deep down in every human heart, there is mercy and generosity.


Human beings have multiple lives and identities within and across racial and ethnic lines.


Let the strivings of us all prove Martin Luther King, Jnr to have been correct when he said that humanity can no longer be tragically bound to the starless midnight of racism and war.


We have fights as human beings, but you should never forget that we are the creation of one Lord.


The world is one stage and the actions of all inhabitants part of the same drama.


None of us can be described as having virtues or qualities that raise him or her above others.

After climbing a great hill, one only finds that there are many more hills to climb.

The universe we inhabit as human beings is becoming a common home that shows growing disrespect for the rigidities imposed on humanity by national boundaries.

Many of us will have to pass through the valley of the shadow of death again and again before we reach the mountain tops of our desires.

## On Imperialism

Imperialism means the denial of political and economic rights and the perpetual subjugation of the people by a foreign power.

Imperialism has been weighed and found
wanting.

## On Inauguration Day, 10 May 1994

One of the outstanding human victories of the
century.

I was overwhelmed with a sense of history.

The time for the healing of the wounds has
come. The moment to bridge the chasms that
divide us has come. The time to build is upon us.

Taken from his Inaugural speech. His inauguration as President of South Africa was
held at the Union Buildings in Pretoria, a day no South African who watched it will
ever forget.

## On India

India's independence was a victory for all people
under colonial rule.

A part of India's soul resides in South Africa as a revered part of our national life.

*He was referring to Mahatma Gandhi.*

## On Islam

Islam has enriched and become part of Africa; in turn, Islam was transformed and Africa became part of it.

## On Jellybeans

What are jellybeans? Are they something that is eaten?

*In a Radio Good Hope interview, May 1996.*

## On Leadership

It is a mistake to think that a single individual can unite the country.

*Swedish radio interview, quoted in the Star, 18 March 1990.*

When leaders have the honesty to criticize their own mistakes and their own organization, then they can criticize others.

There are times when a leader can show sorrow, in public, and that it will not diminish him in the eyes of his people.

*As when he comforted Nomboniso Gasa, who was raped on Robben Island in January 1997. He openly showed his distress and anger.*

Many in positions of power and privilege pursue cold-hearted philosophies which terrifyingly proclaim: I am not your brother's keeper!

*He was speaking to the United Nations in October 1995.*

A leadership commits a crime against its own people if it hesitates to sharpen its political weapons which have become less effective.

It is no use for a leader to surround himself with yes-men.

A leader who relies on authority to solve problems is bound to come to grief.

We have the high salaries and we are living in luxury: that destroys your capacity to speak in a forthright manner and tell people to tighten their belts.

*From an interview on 12 September 1994 – some four months after he was inaugurated as President of South Africa.*

It is important to surround yourself with strong and independent personalities, who will tell you when you are getting old.

Nelson Mandela said this in 1996 when there was speculation about his health, and queries were being raised in South Africa as to whether he would be able to complete his term of office.

It is the fate of leadership to be misunderstood; for historians, academics, writers and journalists to reflect great lives according to their own subjective canon.

A leader who doesn't know when to step down will really come to grief, because he may be humiliated.

## On Liberation

The people are their own liberators.

## On Libya

The people of Libya shared the trenches with us
in our struggle for freedom.

This was said at a banquet in Tripoli, Libya, in October 1997. Nelson Mandela went
to great lengths to get to the pariah country, and was staunch – and even angry – in
the face of American disapproval. One of his mottoes is never to forget a friend – even
if they are held in opprobrium by many.

## On Literature

We could not have made an acquaintance
through literature with human giants such as
George Washington, Abraham Lincoln and
Thomas Jefferson and not have been moved to act
as they were moved to act.

When we read we are able to travel to many
places, meet many people and understand the
world.

## On Love

The world is truly round and seems to start and end with those we love.

*From a letter to Winnie, 1 July 1979.*

I am not nervous of love for love is very inspiring.

*Spoken on his state visit to Britain, July 1996. Only a few people at that time knew of his love for Graça Machel, widow of Samora Machel, first President of Mozambique.*

To be in love is an experience that every man must go through.

One should be so grateful at being involved in such an experience.

I'm in love with a remarkable lady. She has changed my life.

*This was said with a broad smile in a South African television interview in February 1998. He was referring to the much-respected fifty-two-year-old Graça Machel.*

It is such a wonderful period for me.

*Spoken in April 1997, and referring to his relationship with Graça Machel.*

I don't regret the setbacks I have had before and, late in my life, I am blooming like a flower because of her support.

*Again, referring to Graça Machel.*

## On Marriage

The whole purpose of a husband and wife is that when hard times knock at the door you should be able to embrace each other.

According to our custom, you marry the village and not the human being.

A man and wife usually discuss their most
intimate problems in the bedroom.

*Spoken in March 1996, in public, at his divorce hearing from his second wife,
Winnie.*

Ladies don't want to be marrying an old man
like me.

*On being asked whether he would marry Graça Machel (1996).*

## On the Middle East Peace Process

The spurning of agreements reached in good
faith and the forceful occupation of land can only
fan the flames of conflict.

Extremists on all sides thrive, fed by the blood
lust of centuries gone by.

Palestinian and Israeli campaigners for peace
know that security for any nation is not abstract;
neither is it exclusive.

At the end of a century which has seen such a desert of devastation caused by horrific wars, a century which at last has gained much experience in the peaceful resolution of conflicts, we must ask: is this a time for war; is this a time for sending young men to their death?

This was said on his being awarded an Honorary Doctorate by Ben-Gurion University of the Negev, 19 September 1997.

## On Misfortunes

There are few misfortunes in this world that you cannot turn into a personal triumph if you have the iron will and the necessary skill.

## On Morality

A movement without a vision is a movement without moral foundation.

## On the National Party

Where were they when our people died at the hands of the police?

We are hopeful that, in their role, they will add another brick into the edifice of our young democracy.

For people that had to invoke the name of God as they made our people suffer? For people who warped the concept of Christianity to cloak the abomination of apartheid in it?

*Incredulously referring to the National Party, the bulwark of apartheid until 1994, versus the South African Communist Party.*

Even with all their bombers and tanks, they must have sensed they were on the wrong side of history.

## On Negotiation

Concessions are inherent in negotiations.

It is difficult to negotiate with those who do not share the same frame of reference.

When you negotiate you have to accept the integrity of another man.

When you negotiate you must be prepared to compromise.

Negotiated solutions can be found even to conflicts that have come to seem intractable and that such solutions emerge when those who have been divided reach out to find the common ground. .

Only free men can negotiate.

*He wrote this in a letter to then State President P.W. Botha, dismissing with contempt Botha's offer of conditional release. And although it was illegal for Mandela's words to be repeated in South Africa, his letter was defiantly read out to the crowds by his youngest daughter, Zindzi, at Jabulani Stadium, Soweto, on 10 February 1985. He had another five years of imprisonment to go.*

## On the New World Order

Is the time not upon us when we should cease to treat tyranny, instability and poverty anywhere on our globe as being peripheral to our interests and to our future?

Can we say with confidence that it is within our reach to declare that never again shall continents, countries or communities be reduced to the smoking battlefields of contending forces of nationality, religion, race or language?

*From his lecture at the Oxford Centre for Islamic Studies, 11 July 1997.*

Intervention only works when the people concerned seem to be keen for peace.

e world frees itself from the dominance of
.. lar power the stark division of the world's
people into rich and poor comes all the more
clearly into view.

If I have any moral authority – and I say if –
moral authority doesn't solve world problems.

The reality can no longer be ignored that we live
in an interdependent world which is bound
together to a common destiny.

We operate in a world which is searching for a
better life – without the imprisonment of dogma.

Let us join hands to ensure that as we enter the
new millennium, the political rights that the
twentieth century has recognized, and the
independence that nations have gained, shall be
translated into peace, prosperity and equity for
all.

As the process of globalization grows apace, so does the system of international governance also grow stronger.

## On the Nobel Peace Prize

Let it never be said by future generations that indifference, cynicism or selfishness made us fail to live up to the ideals of humanism which the Nobel Peace Prize encapsulates.

Nobel Peace Prize ceremony, Oslo, Norway, 10 December 1993. He received the award jointly with F.W. de Klerk, at that time still State President of South Africa. The Nobel Peace Prize had a special meaning to him, because his award was preceded by two other South Africans: Chief Albert Luthuli, former president of the ANC was a Nobel Peace Prize winner, as was Archbishop Desmond Tutu.

I assumed the Nobel Committee would never consider for the peace prize the man who had started Umkhonto we Sizwe.

*Umkhonto we Sizwe, or Spear of the Nation, was the military wing of the ANC, formed by Nelson Mandela in June 1961. Arguing his case, he said: 'Sebatana ha se bokwe ka diatla' ('The attacks of the wild beast cannot be averted with only bare hands').*

## On Oppression

To overthrow oppression has been sanctioned by humanity and is the highest aspiration of every free man.

*From his famous 'No Easy Walk To Freedom' speech, 1953.*

For as long as legitimate bodies of opinion feel stifled, vile minds will take advantage of justifiable grievances to destroy, to kill and to maim.

I haven't suffered to the same extent other people have whilst I was relaxing in prison.

For as long as the majority of people anywhere on the continent [of Africa] feel oppressed, are not allowed democratic participation in decision-making processes, and cannot elect their own leaders in free and fair elections, there will always be tension and conflict.

Never and never again shall the laws of our land rend our people apart or legalize their oppression and repression.

## On His Parents

My father was a polygamist with four wives and nine children.

My mother was my first friend in the proper sense of the word.

The graves mean a great deal to me because my beloved parents are here and it arouses a great deal of emotion in me because part of myself lies buried here.

*He was standing next to his parents' simple graves in Qunu. His mother died while he was on Robben Island and the authorities denied him permission to attend her funeral. The first time he was able to pay his respects to her was after his release from prison in 1990.*

## On Peace

Peace and democracy go hand in hand.

It is not easy to talk about peace to people who are mourning every day.

I will go down on my knees to beg those who want to drag our country into bloodshed and persuade them not to do so.

Everyone must fight for peace.

To some, talking about peace is a sign of cowardice – but in fact it is a sign of strength.

Peace is its own reward.

Peace and prosperity, tranquillity and security are only possible if these are enjoyed by all without discrimination.

## On People

I love you. You are my own flesh and blood. You are my brothers, sisters, children and grandchildren.

*Speaking to the people of South Africa.*

I surely wish the pockets of my shirt were big enough to fit all of you in.

*To his compatriots in the Transkei.*

In life, every man has twin obligations —
obligations to his family, to his parents, to his
wife and children; and he has an obligation to his
people, his community and his country.

Language, culture and religion are important
indicators of identity.

Justice and liberty must be our tool, prosperity
and happiness our weapon.

It is in the character of growth that we should
learn from both pleasant and unpleasant
experiences.

The suffering of the people of any single country
affects all of us no matter where we find
ourselves.

## On the People of the World

[I am] an old man who loves you all from the
bottom of his heart.

## On Personalities

### Steve Biko, murdered black consciousness activist

There can be no doubt that he was one of the
most talented and colourful freedom fighters
South Africa has produced.

One of the greatest sons of our nation.

That he was indeed a great man who stood head
and shoulders above his peers is borne out not
only by the testimony of those who knew him
and worked with him, but by the fruit of his
endeavours.

A fitting product of his time; a proud
representative of the re-awakening of a people.

### P.W. Botha, former State President

The thing that impressed me was that he poured
the tea.

*After their first meeting, 4 July 1989. Mandela was still behind bars in Cape Town's
Pollsmoor Prison. So unused was he to shoes with laces, that one of his captors had to
tie them for him.*

I will never allow him to defy the TRC.

*In spite of Mandela's efforts, their relationship has curdled, with Botha's refusal, at the
end of 1997, to appear before South Africa's Truth and Reconciliation Commission
(TRC).*

### Mangosuthu Buthelezi, IFP President, and Minister of Home Affairs

When we are together, he is very, very
courteous. But when he is away from you, he
behaves totally differently, because he does not
know if he is still your friend or not.

The problem is when he leaves the cabinet and
appears on public platforms. Then he behaves
like any other politician.

## Prince Charles

This is a real king, not the Lion King.

*Nelson Mandela's grandchildren were being introduced to Prince Charles during his historic official visit to South Africa, October 1997. The Prince of Wales was accompanied by his younger son, Prince Harry.*

## Bill Clinton, US President

There is a vow of goodwill between us.

## F.W. de Klerk, former State President

He had the courage to admit that a terrible wrong had been done to our country and people through the imposition of the system of apartheid.

Despite his seemingly progressive actions, Mr de Klerk was by no means the great emancipator.

If there is anything that has cooled relations between me and Mr de Klerk, it is his paralysis as far as violence is concerned.

*This was said in September 1992, with reference to the Boipatong massacre and the increasingly inexplicable 'third force' violence in South Africa; in view of Mr de Klerk's much criticized submissions to the Truth and Reconciliation Commission, it was a prophetic remark.*

### Diana, Princess of Wales

I found her very graceful, highly intelligent and committed to worthy causes, and I was tremendously impressed by her warmness.

[She] became a citizen of the world through her care for people everywhere.

*He said this at the state banquet for Prince Charles held in Cape Town, on 4 November 1997.*

### Queen Elizabeth II

The Queen is a very gracious lady and I'm sure she'll put a country boy at ease.

*On the eve of his historic – and jubilant – state visit to Britain, July 1996.*

## Mahatma Gandhi

It would not be right to compare me to Gandhi.
None of us could equal his dedication or his
humility.

He showed us that it was necessary to brave
imprisonment if truth and justice were to
triumph over evil.

We must never lose sight of the fact that the
Gandhian philosophy may be a key to human
survival in the twenty-first century.

## Jose Xana Gusmão, imprisoned East Timorese leader

It was regrettable that a man of his talents should
languish in jail.

There are poignant similarities between Gusmão's plight and that of Mandela. Gusmão
has been sentenced to prison for twenty years for opposing the Indonesian invasion of
his country; his latter-day champion is Nelson Mandela.

## Chris Hani, assassinated leader of the ANC Youth League

A white man, full of prejudice and hate, came to our country and committed a deed so foul that our whole nation now teeters on the brink of disaster. A white woman, of Afrikaner origin, risked her life so that we might know, and bring to justice, this assassin.

*Speech to all South Africans, calming the angry youth after Hani's assassination at the hands of a white man (10 April 1992).*

## Bishop Trevor Huddleston

His sacrifices for our freedom told us that the true relationship between our people was not one between poor citizens on the one hand and good patricians on the other, but one underwritten by our common humanity and our human capacity to touch one another's hearts across the oceans.

### Martin Luther King, Jnr

He grappled with and died in the effort to make a contribution to the just solution of the same great issues of the day which we have had to face as South Africans.

From his Nobel Peace Prize address, 10 December 1993.


### Sophia Loren

I would never miss a movie with Sophia Loren in it.


### Thabo Mbeki, Deputy President

He is polite but he is not a yes-man. He will always stand his ground.

Whilst I was fighting warders in jail, he was meeting heads of state and there learnt the art of diplomacy.

He is a man of exceptional quality, very respectful, very warm.

## General Colin Powell, former Chief of the Defence Staff

I won't wash this hand you have shaken.

*It was a mutual admiration session: Colin Powell had just said: 'This is truly a very great honour for me.'*


## Cyril Ramaphosa, trade unionist, politician, negotiator and businessman

He is a son to me.

A young man of considerable ability destined to occupy a very important position in our political life.


## Oliver Tambo, former President of the ANC

When I looked at him in his coffin, it was as if a part of myself had died.

*Oliver Tambo was Nelson Mandela's lifelong friend. They were in law practice together. Later on the head of the ANC, Tambo lived most of his life in exile. He returned to South Africa but died shortly afterwards, not living long enough to see his dream of a democratic South Africa realized.*

He is my greatest friend and comrade for fifty years.

He enriched my own life and intellect, and neither I nor indeed this country [South Africa] can forget this colossus of our history.

*Archbishop Desmond Tutu, Nobel laureate*

He has been a blessing and inspiration to countless people through his ministry, his acts of compassion, his prophetic witness and his political engagement.

Said at the thanksgiving service for the ministry of Archbishop Tutu in Cape Town, June 1996.

He's a terrific fellow.

## On Photography

Good use of photography will give even poverty with all its rags, filth and vermin a measure of divineness rarely noticeable in real life.

From a letter to Zindzi, 6 August 1979.

## On Politics

Political power should be the basis for the economic empowerment of people.
We should not allow South African politics to be relegated to trivialities chosen precisely because they salve the consciences of the rich and powerful, and conceal the plight of the poor and powerless.

If you are a politician you must be prepared to suffer for your principles.

Political division, based on colour, is entirely artificial and, when it disappears, so will the domination of one colour group by another.

From the dock at the Rivonia Treason Trial, 20 April 1964.

A political movement must keep in touch with reality.

## On Poverty

It should never be that the anger of the poor
should be the finger of accusation pointed at all
of us because we failed to respond to the cries of
the people for food, for shelter, for the dignity of
the individual.

None can be at peace while others wallow in
poverty and insecurity.

## On Praise

The exaltation of the President, and denigration
of other ANC leaders, constitutes praise which I
do not accept.

# On Being President (of South Africa)

This has placed a great responsibility on my shoulders.

At the end of my term I'll be eighty-one. I don't think it's wise that a robust country like South Africa should be led by a septuagenarian.

*Spoken in 1996 when there were rumours about his health. A septuagenarian when he made the comment, he would, of course, be an octogenarian at the end of his term of office.*

It is a way of life in which it's hard to dedicate time to the things that are really close to your heart.

To be the father of a nation is a great honour, but to be the father of a family is a greater joy.

My present life, even if it's not the easiest way of life, is very rewarding.

*Spoken in mid 1997, one of his busiest years.*

## On the Press

A critical, independent and investigative press is the lifeblood of any democracy.

It was the press who never forgot us.
*Spoken just after his February 1990 release.*

A press conference is not a place to discuss rumours.

It is only a free press that can temper the appetite of any government to amass power at the expense of the citizen.

## On Prison

Nothing is more dehumanizing than isolation
from human companionship.

*Nelson Mandela saw Robben Island for the first time from Table Mountain, Cape
Town, in 1947. Less than twenty years later, he was incarcerated there.*

The long, lonely wasted years.

*He was prisoner 466/64.*

I believe the way in which you are treated by the
prison authorities depends on your demeanour
and you must fight that battle and win it on the
very first day.

There I had time, just to sit for hours and think.

## On Racism

I detest racialism, because I regard it as a barbaric thing, whether it comes from a black man or a white man.

Racism pollutes the atmosphere of human relations and poisons the minds of the backward, the bigoted and the prejudiced.

Our struggle is the struggle to erase the colour line that all too often determines who is rich and who is poor.

As we enter the last decade of the twentieth century, it is intolerable and unacceptable that the cancer of racism is still eating away at the fabric of societies in different parts of our planet.

We must ensure that colour, race and gender become only a God-given gift to each one of us and not an indelible mark or attribute that accords a special status to any.

We shall never again allow our country to play host to racism. Nor shall our voices be stilled if we see that another, elsewhere in the world, is victim to racial tyranny.

Racism must be consciously combated and not discreetly tolerated.

The very fact that racism degrades both the perpetrator and the victim commands that, if we are true to our commitment to protect human dignity, we fight on until victory is achieved.

All of us know how stubbornly racism can cling to the mind and how deeply it can infect the human soul.

I hate the practice of race discrimination, and in my hatred I am sustained by the fact that the over-whelming majority of mankind hate it equally.

Racism is a blight on the human conscience.

Death to racism.

## On Reconciliation

The mission of reconciliation is underpinned by what I have dedicated my life to: uplifting the most downtrodden sections of our population and all-round transformation of society.

We need to reconcile our differences through reason, debate and compromise.

Without reconciliation, we will not be able to give our people a better life.

Above all the healing process involves the nation, because it is the nation itself that needs to redeem and reconstruct itself.

Reconstruction goes hand in hand with reconciliation.

We can easily be enticed to read reconciliation and fairness as meaning parity between justice and injustice.

The first founding stone of our new country is national reconciliation and national unity. The fact that it has settled in its mortar needs no advertising.

## On Regina Mundi

A church that refused to allow God's name to be used to justify discrimination and repression.

Regina Mundi is a simple, red brick cathedral in Soweto, frequently the focus of defiance during the struggle, and symbolic to many of defiance and the fight for freedom.

A literal battlefield between forces of democracy and those who did not hesitate to violate a place of religion with tear-gas, dogs and guns.

Regina Mundi became a worldwide symbol of
the determination of our people to free
themselves.

The people's cathedral.

## On His Release

I greet you all in the name of peace, democracy
and freedom for all.

Historic words indeed; he said them to the wildly excited crowd as he walked out of
Victor Verster Prison, Paarl, holding the hand of his then wife Winnie on 11
February 1990. He was seventy-one.

I would be merely rationalizing if I told you that
I am able to describe my own feelings. It was
breathtaking, that is all I can say.

Along the route [from Paarl to Cape Town] I was
surprised to see the number of whites who
seemed to identify themselves with what is
happening to the country today amongst blacks.

I was completely overwhelmed by the
enthusiasm.

## On Religion

The simple lesson of religions, of all philosophies
and of life itself is that, although evil may be on
the rampage temporarily, the good must win the
laurels in the end.

*From a letter to his friend, Fatima Meer, 1 January 1976. Less than six months
later, the Soweto uprising broke out, signalling the eventual end of apartheid.*

Religion runs in our veins.

*Referring to South Africans.*

The strength of inter-religious solidarity in action
against apartheid, rather than mere harmony or
co-existence, was critical in bringing that evil
system to an end.

[African traditional religion] is no longer seen as despised superstition which had to be superseded by superior forms of belief; today its enrichment of humanity's spiritual heritage is acknowledged.

We need religious institutions to continue to be the conscience of society, a moral custodian and a fearless champion of the interests of the weak and downtrodden.

## On Retirement

I must step down while there are one or two people who admire me.

November 1996, when he was seventy-eight.

I intend to do a bit of farming when I step down. I will be without a job and I don't want to find myself standing at the side of the road with a placard saying: unemployed.

There is no reason whatsoever for anyone to think there will be dislocation in South Africa as a result of the stepping down of an individual.

I look forward to the period when I will be able to wake up with the sun, to walk the hills and valleys of Qunu in peace and tranquillity.

*Nelson Mandela has often spoken of Qunu with longing. On this occasion it was especially so. This was the final sentence in his 'private' (as opposed to his controversial five hour 'political') speech at the historic fiftieth ANC conference held in Mafikeng in December 1997, when he relinquished his presidency of the ANC and clearly looked ahead towards his retirement in 1999.*

I will be able to have that opportunity in my last years to spoil my grandchildren and try in various ways to assist all South African children, especially those who have been the hapless victims of a system that did not care.

My retirement will give me the opportunity to sit down with my children and grandchildren and listen to their dreams and to help them as much as possible.

I will still go into Shell House on Mondays and carry out whatever instructions my president gives me.

Shell House, the ANC headquarters, is in the heart of Johannesburg; his president, president of the ANC that is, from mid December 1997, is Thabo Mbeki.

## On His Retirement as President of the ANC

The time has come to hand over the baton in a relay that started more than eighty-five years ago in Mangaung; nay more, centuries ago when the warriors of the Autshumanyo, Makhanda, Mzilikazi, Moshoeshoe, Khama, Sekhukhune, Lobatsibeni, Cetshwayo, Nghunghunyane, Uithalder and Ramabulana, laid down their loves to defend the dignity and integrity of their being as a people.

Here are the reins of the movement – protect and guard its precious legacy.

I know that the love and respect that I have enjoyed is love and respect for the ANC and its ideals.

I will remember this experience fondly for as long as I live.

The time has come for me to take leave.

*All the above quotations were taken from Nelson Mandela's valedictory address to the closing session of the historic fiftieth national conference of the ANC on 20 December 1997. As the speech drew to its conclusion, he had tears in his eyes.*

## On Revenge

You can't build a united nation on the basis of revenge.

*In an interview with The New York Times in March 1997; he was referring to the Truth and Reconciliation Commission.*

## On the South African Right Wing

There are still powerful elements among whites
who are not reconciled with the present
transformation and who want to use every excuse
to drown the country in bloodshed.

*He said this in 1996, repeating the assertion in December 1997 in his speech at the
fiftieth ANC Congress in Mafikeng.*

There are still some within our country who
wrongly believe they can make a contribution to
the cause of justice and peace by clinging to the
shibboleths that have been proved to spell
nothing but disaster.

## On Robben Island

Siqithini – the Island – a place of pain and
banishment for centuries, and now of triumph.

*He was speaking on Heritage Day, 24 September 1997, on Robben Island itself.*

Without question the harshest, most iron-fisted outpost in the South African penal system.

*Robben Island, nine kilometres off the Cape coast and set in the tumultuous Atlantic Ocean, has been used as a prison for hundreds of years – the first prisoner was Harry the Strandloper, confined there by the Dutch in 1658. But Robben Island is no longer a prison – it has been turned into a museum and can be visited by anyone. Mandela revisited his former prison on 11 February 1994, posing in his old cell in B Section, and showing the world the limestone quarry in which he and his fellow prisoners had worked year after year.*

A symbol of the victory of the human spirit over political oppression, and of reconciliation over enforced division.

The Island has become a monument of the struggle for democracy, part of a heritage that will always inspire our children and our friends from other lands.

## On Rwanda

Rwanda stands out as a stern and severe rebuke to all of us.

The louder and more piercing the cries of despair – even when that despair results in half a million dead in Rwanda – the more these cries seem to encourage an instinctive reaction to raise our hands so as to close our eyes and ears.

None of us can insulate ourselves from so catastrophic a scale of human suffering.

# On the Rugby World Cup, South Africa, 1995

Our whole nation stood behind a sport which was once a symbol of apartheid.

*None more so than Nelson Mandela himself. He appeared at the final wearing captain François Pienaar's No. 6 shirt — and brought the entire country along with him, surely one of the most successful efforts at reconciliation in South Africa.*

When it was 12–12 I almost collapsed. I was absolutely tense.

When I left the stadium my nerves were completely shattered.

*South Africa won an historic and nationally popular victory after a nail-biting climax.*

I'm still recovering.

*Two years later, in 1997!*

## On Sabotage

I planned it as a result of a calm and sober
assessment of the situation, after many years of
oppression and tyranny of my people by the
whites.

From the Rivonia Treason Trial, 20 April 1964 – the trial which sent him to prison
for twenty-seven years.

## On Self-respect

If you are in harmony with yourself, you may
meet a lion without fear, because he respects
anyone with self-confidence.

## On Soccer

Soccer is one of the sporting disciplines in which
Africa is rising to demonstrate her excellence, for
too long latent in her womb.

## On Society

The great lesson of our time is that no regime can survive if it acts above the heads of the ordinary citizens of the country.

Through persuasion, and in line with the constitution, we should together build a democratic and prosperous society, at peace with itself.

## On South Africa

We are marching to a new future based on a sound basis of respect.

We live with the hope that as she battles to remake herself, South Africa will be like a microcosm of the new world that is striving to be born.

From his Nobel Peace Prize address, 10 December 1993.

Each time one of us touches the soil of this land, we feel a sense of personal renewal.

Never and never again shall it be that this beautiful land will again experience the oppression of one by another and suffer the indignity of being the skunk of the world.

From his moving Inauguration speech, 10 May 1994.

No society emerging out of the grand disaster of the apartheid system could avoid carrying the blemishes of its past.

If we are able today to speak proudly of a 'rainbow nation', it is in part because the world set us a moral example which we dared to follow.

Should [we not] begin to define the national interest to include the genuine happiness of others, however distant in time and space their domicile might be?

Had the new South Africa emerged out of
nothing, it would not exist.

We do face major challenges, but none are as
daunting as those we have already surmounted.

On receiving the Freedom of the City of London, July 1996.

We must work for the day when we, as South
Africans, see one another and interact with one
another as equal human beings and as part of one
nation united, rather than torn asunder, by its
diversity.

Being latecomers to freedom and democracy, we
have the benefit of the experience of others.

In the same way that the liberation of South
Africa from apartheid was an achievement of
Africa, the reconstruction and development of
our country is part of the rebirth of the
continent.

The hard slog of reconstruction and development is as exciting as the tremors of conflict.

South Africa is a worldwide icon of the universality of human rights; of hope, peace and reconciliation.

In time, we must bestow on South Africa the greatest gift – a more humane society.

What we have achieved will serve as a symbol of peace and reconciliation, and of hope, wherever communities and societies are in the grip of conflict.

## On South Africans

We are all one nation in one country.

We enter into a covenant that we shall build a society in which all South Africans, both black and white, will be able to walk tall, without any fear in their hearts, assured of their inalienable right to human dignity – a rainbow nation at peace with itself and the world.

From his Inauguration speech, 10 May 1994.


Each one of us is as intimately attached to the soil of this beautiful country as are the famous jacaranda trees of Pretoria and the mimosa trees of the bushveld.

From his Inauguration speech, 10 May 1994.


My country is rich in the minerals and gems that lie beneath its soil, but I have always known that its greatest wealth is its people, finer and truer than the purest diamonds.


It is our privilege as South Africans to be living at a time when our nation is emerging from the darkest night into the bright dawn of freedom and democracy.

Pride in our country is a common bond between us all. It is the essence of our new patriotism.

The onus is on us, through hard work, honesty and integrity, to reach for the stars.

With all our colours and races combined in one nation, we are an African people.

Having achieved our own freedom, we can fall into the trap of washing our hands of difficulties that others face.

No South African should rest and wallow in the joy of freedom.

## On Sport

Sport can reach out to people in a way which politicians can't.

## On the Struggle

The Struggle is my life.

From his famous press statement of 26 June 1961, whilst living underground as the Black Pimpernel.

It is always the oppressor, not the oppressed, who dictates the form of the struggle.

Struggle that does not strengthen organization can lead to a blind alley.

Struggle without unity enables the other side to pick us off one by one.

A willingness to make sacrifices for a loftier purpose was the unwritten code of the struggle.

[South Africans] displayed heroism, an incredible sense of discipline and a capacity for selflessness, as well as a quiet determination not to bend the knee to the dictates of tyrants.

Running through the struggle like a golden thread
is one motif – the indomitable human spirit and
a moving capacity for self-sacrifice and discipline.

Struggle without discipline can lead to anarchy.

## On Survival

For me, survival is the ability to cope with difficulties, with circumstances, and to overcome them.

## On Sweden

We have become political neighbours who
willingly share whatever little bread and salt we
may have.

## On Talk

Rhetoric is not important. Actions are.

## On Time

A lack of punctuality is something which shows lack of respect for the organization and those appointed into positions, and a lack of self-respect.

## On Tolerance

You should be tolerant to those who have views that are different to yours, because you will win by the correctness of the position that you take.

## On Truth

No matter how hard its adversary – falsehood –
may try to overwhelm it, truth refuses to yield.

I am prepared to stand by the truth even if
everyone is against me.

## On the Truth and Reconciliation Commission

Above all the healing process involved the nation,
because it is the nation itself that needs to redeem
and reconstruct itself.

The Truth and Reconciliation Commission started its work in February 1996. It has
heard of atrocities from the right and the left, has heard testimony from murderers and
torturers – and also from victims and the families of dead victims. It is intended to be
an instrument of reconciliation and not revenge.

All South Africans face the challenge of coming to terms with the past in ways which will enable us to face the future as a united nation at peace with itself.

Some criticize us when we say that whilst we can forgive, we can never forget.

Ordinary South Africans are determined that the past be known, the better to ensure that it is not repeated.

Incomplete and imperfect as the process may be, it shall leave us less burdened by the past and unshackled to pursue a glorious future.

This was said in his New Year's message to South Africa, 31 December 1997; it followed a harrowing year at the Truth and Reconciliation Commission, where the country's brutal past was ripped open for all to see. One of the last people called to give evidence before the Commission in 1997 was Winnie Madikizela-Mandela, the President's second wife.

We are all bound to agonize over the price in terms of justice that the victims have to pay.

The half-truths of a lowly interrogator cannot
and should not hide the culpability of the
commanders and the political leaders who gave
the orders.

South Africa's apartheid leaders failed abysmally before the TRC to take responsibility
for the actions of their foot soldiers or for the overall policies and abuses of apartheid.

## On Ubuntu

The spirit of ubuntu, that profound African sense
that we are human only through the humanity of
other human beings – is not a parochial
phenomenon, but has added globally to our
common search for a better world.

There are numerous definitions of ubuntu – kindness towards human beings is
perhaps too mild; as Mandela says, it is to do with one's humanity being enriched by
another's.

## On the United Kingdom

I regard the British parliament as the most democratic institution in the world, and the independence and impartiality of its judiciary never fail to arouse my admiration.

From the Rivonia Treason Trail, 20 April 1964.


Your right to determine your own destiny was used to deny us to determine our own.

From his speech to the House of Commons, 5 May 1993.


This country has produced men and women whose names are well known in South Africa, because they, together with thousands of others of your citizens, stood up to oppose this evil system and helped to bring us to where we are today.


We return to this honoured place neither with pikes nor a desire for revenge nor even a plea to your distinguished selves to assuage our hunger for bread. We come to you as friends.

*From his historic speech to both Houses of Parliament, London, July 1996.*


In a sense, I leave a part of my being here.

*Receiving the Freedom of the City of London, July 1996.*


The UK, as one of the bastions of democracy, has an obligation to ensure that we have all the material needs to entrench democracy in our country.


I love every one of you. You must understand that the people of South Africa are very grateful to you.

*Addressing a crowd of 10,000 from the balcony of South Africa House, Trafalgar Square, London, July 1996.*

# On the USA

We are linked by nature, but proud of each other by choice.

*Of New York, which he visited with Winnie on his first trip abroad after his February 1990 release, he said: 'To see it from the bottom of its great glass-and-concrete canyons while millions upon millions of pieces of ticker tape came floating down was a breathtaking experience.'*

The stand you took established the understanding among the millions of our people that here we have friends, here we have fighters against racism who feel hurt because we are hurt, who seek our success because they too seek the victory of democracy over tyranny.

*Address to the joint Houses of Congress of the USA, Washington, DC, September 1994.*

Let us keep our arms locked together so that we form a solid phalanx against racism.

You have felt and recognized that our success advances the very principles on which this country is founded.

## On Violence

Take your guns, your knives and your pangas,
and throw them into the sea.

His first speech in the troubled province of KwaZulu/Natal after his release from
prison, 25 February 1990.

People who kill children are no better than
animals.

In the end, the cries of the infant who dies
because of hunger or because a machete has slit
open its stomach, will penetrate the noises of the
modern city and its sealed windows to say: am I
not human too!

From his speech to both Houses of Parliament, London, 11 July 1996.

Use violence only in self-defence.

## On Virtue

Virtue and generosity will be rewarded in ways that one cannot know.

## On the Vote

On numerous occasions it has been proven in history that people can enjoy the vote even if they have no education.

A vote without food, shelter and health care would be to create the appearance of equality while actual inequality is entrenched.

The question of education has nothing to do with the question of the vote.

*As in Zimbabwe, there was a vocal section of white voters who maintained that the vote should not be given to uneducated or barely literate people. Some form of qualification, resulting in a limited franchise, was suggested. This was rejected – as it had been in Zimbabwe – for one man, one vote.*

## On White South Africans

The majority of white men regard it as the destiny of the white race to dominate the man of colour.

*From the ANC Youth League Manifesto of 1944, largely written by him.*

White supremacy implies black inferiority.

*From the dock at the Rivonia Treason Trial, 20 April 1964.*

Just as many whites have killed just as many blacks.

*Asked about deaths of white civilians in ANC attacks, 1990.*

Whites fear the reality of democracy.

As long as whites think in terms of group rights they are talking the language of apartheid.

*Spoken before the elections in April 1994.*

Whites are fellow South Africans and we want them to feel safe, and we appreciate the contribution they have made towards the development of this country.

They have had education, they have got the knowledge, skills and expertise. We want that knowledge and expertise now that we are building our country.

# On *Winnie*

I had hoped to build you a refuge, no matter
how small, so that we would have a place for rest
and sustenance before the arrival of the sad, dry
days.

From a letter to Winnie from Robben Island, 26 June 1977.

Had it not been for your visits, wonderful letters
and your love, I would have fallen apart many
years ago.

From a letter to Winnie, 6 May 1979.

I have often wondered whether any kind of
commitment can ever be sufficient excuse for
abandoning a young and inexperienced woman
in a pitiless desert.

Letter to Winnie, 1985.

I cannot say for certain if there is such a thing as
love at first sight, but I do know that the moment
I first glimpsed Winnie Nomzamo, I knew that I
wanted to have her as my wife.

They were married on 15 June 1958.

I am convinced that your pain and suffering was far greater than my own.

From his first speech as a free man, Cape Town, 11 February 1990.

She married a man who soon left her; that man became a myth; and then that myth returned home and proved to be just a man after all.

In a curiously similar turn of phrase, Graça Machel, widow of President Samora Machel of Mozambique, and Nelson Mandela's companion since 1996, said of him in an interview at the beginning of 1998: 'I found this very simple man who appeared so humble, so soft, so common. It was a conflict between myth and the reality.'

I embrace her with all the love and affection I have nursed for her inside and outside prison from the moment I first met her.

Announcing his separation from Winnie, 13 April 1992.

My love for her remains undiminished.

Part of his poignant separation announcement.

I was the loneliest man during the period I stayed with her.

During his divorce trial, March 1996.

## On Women

The beauty of a woman lies as much in her face as in her body.

*From a letter to his daughter Zindzi, 5 March 1978.*

If a pretty woman walks by, I don't want to be out of the running.

*An aside at a dinner to foreign correspondent Patti Waldmeir.*

Women today are very sensitive to men expressing opinions without consulting them.

*He said this to a persistent reporter asking him when he was going to marry the then absent Graça Machel.*

Freedom cannot be achieved unless women have been emancipated from all forms of oppression.

## On Work

The people who work must enjoy the fruits of their labour.

Jobs, jobs and jobs are the dividing line in many families between a decent life and a wretched existence.

Workers need a living wage – and the right to join unions of their own choice and to participate in determining policies that affect their lives.

## On Writing

Writing is a prestigious profession which puts one right into the centre of the world and, to remain on top, one has to work really hard, the aim being a good and original theme, simplicity in expression and the use of the irreplaceable word.

From a letter to his daughter Zindzi, 4 September 1977.

## On Youth

I admire young people who are concerned with
the affairs of their community and nation perhaps
because I also became involved in struggle whilst
I was still at school.

Young people are capable, when aroused, of
bringing down the towers of oppression and
raising the banners of freedom.

I appeal to the youth and all those on the ground:
start talking to each other across divisions of race
and political organizations.

I pay tribute to the endless heroism of youth.

Whenever I am with energetic young people, I
feel like a recharged battery.

## On Zulus

No people can boast more proudly of having ploughed a significant field in the struggle.

Zulus have fought a long struggle against oppression.

The Battle of Isandlwana in 1879 has been an inspiration for those of us engaged in the struggle for justice and freedom in South Africa.

The battle took place under a midday eclipse on 22 January 1879; some 20,000 Zulu warriors swept across the Nqutu plateau and, after scenes of heroism and desperation on both sides, defeated the vastly outnumbered British and colonial troops camped beneath the mountain of Isandlwana. The Zulus were, in effect, fighting invaders on their soil, the Anglo-Zulu war being a shamefully trumped-up affair. On the night of the battle, part of the Zulu army went on to attack Rorke's Drift. The tiny garrison withstood the onslaught, earning for its defenders eleven Victoria Crosses. A few months later, British troops fired the Zulu capital, Ulundi, captured the king, Cetshwayo, and brought the proud nation to its knees.

When my sentence has been completed I will still be moved, as men are always moved, by their consciences; I will still be moved by my dislike of the race discrimination against my people when I come out from serving my sentence, to take up again, as best I can, the struggle for the removal of those injustices until they are finally abolished once and for all.

*Spoken in court, on 7 November 1962, at the end of the Old Synagogue trial when he was convicted and sentenced to three years' imprisonment on charges of incitement and two years' imprisonment for leaving South Africa without valid travel documents.*

# Sources

Mary Benson, *Nelson Mandela: The Man and the Movement*
(Penguin, Harmondsworth, 1994)

H.H.W. de Villiers, *Rivonia — Operation Mayibuye: A Review
of the Rivonia Trial* (Afrikaanse Pers Boekhandel,
Johannesburg, 1964)

*The Historic Speech of Nelson Rolihlahla Mandela at the Rivonia
Trial* (Learn and Teach Publications, Johannesburg,
1964)

Nelson Mandela, *The Struggle is My Life* (Pathfinder, New
York, 1991)

Fatima Meer, *Higher Than Hope* (Penguin,
Harmondsworth, 1990)

Patti Waldmeir, *Anatomy of a Miracle* (Viking, London,
1997)

ANC Youth League Manifesto, 1944; Associated Press;
*Argus*; *Business Day*; *Cape Times*; *Citizen*; *Daily Telegraph*;
*Financial Times*; *Liberation*; *Mail & Guardian*; *Natal Witness*; *The
New York Times*; *RSA Review* 1995; SAPA; *Saturday Star*;
*Sowetan*; *Sunday Independent*; *Sunday Telegraph*; *Sunday Times*;
*Time*; *Vogue* (French edition), December 1993/January
1994

Radio Good Hope; Radio 702; M-Net; SABC;
'Shifting Sands of Illusion' article, *Liberation*, June
1953; 'No Easy Walk to Freedom' speech,
21 September 1953; 'Freedom in Our Lifetime'
article, *Liberation*, June 1956; 'A New Menace in Africa'
article, *Liberation*, March 1958; Prime Minister Dr H.F.
Verwoerd's 'Tribalism' speech, May 1959; 'The
Struggle is My Life' press statement, 26 June 1961;
letter to the Prime Minister, Dr H.F. Verwoerd,
26 June 1961; address to the Conference of the Pan-
African Freedom Movement of East and South Africa,
Addis Ababa, January 1962; 'Black Man in a White
Court' trial speech, the Old Synagogue, Pretoria,
7 November 1962; Rivonia Treason Trial speech,
20 April 1964; letter to his daughter Zindzi Mandela,
4 September 1977; 'Mandela's Call to the Youth of
South Africa' smuggled speech, 1980; 'Whilst Still in
Prison', his first speech in almost twenty-five years,
defiantly read by Zindzi Mandela, 10 February 1985;
release from Victor Verster Prison speech, Cape Town,
11 February 1990; Bishopscourt press conference,
12 February 1990; FNB Stadium (Soccer City) speech,
Johannesburg, 13 February 1990; Bloemfontein
speech, 25 February 1990; Durban Rally speech,
25 February 1990; address to the Swedish Parliament,
13 March 1990; Harlem speech, New York City,
21 June 1990; address to the Joint Session of the
Houses of Congress of the USA, Washington, DC,
26 June 1990; announcement of his separation from

Winnie, 13 April 1992; Gandhi Hall, Lenasia, speech, 27 September 1992; speech to the House of Commons, London, 5 May 1993; acceptance address at the Clark University Investiture, Atlanta, 10 July 1993; Nobel Peace Prize award ceremony speech, Oslo, 10 December 1993; ANC election victory speech, 2 May 1994; Inauguration speech, 10 May 1994; address to the forty-ninth session of the United Nations General Assembly, New York City, 3 October 1994; Business Leaders speech, New Delhi, India, 26 January 1995; African Cup of Nations Tournament speech, 13 January 1996; Interfaith Commissioning Service for the Truth and Reconciliation Commission speech, 13 February 1996; University of Potchefstroom speech, 19 February 1996; opening of South African Parliament speech, 9 February 1996; Thanksgiving Service for the Ministry of Archbishop Tutu, Cape Town, 23 June 1996; South African Representatives to Olympic and Paralympic Games, Atlanta, speech, 28 June 1996; OAU Summit speech, Yaounde, Cameroon, 8 July 1996; Freedom of the City of London, Guildhall speech, 10 July 1996; Joint Houses of Parliament speech, London, 11 July 1996; Bastille Day speech, Paris, 14 July 1996; seventy-fifth anniversary of the South African Communist Party speech, 28 July 1996; Warrenton Presidential School Project speech, 30 August 1996; signing of the South African Constitution speech, Sharpeville, 10 December 1996; 'Food for Life', Pietermaritzburg speech,

23 April 1997; Freedom of Pietermaritzburg speech,
25 April 1997; state banquet speech for President
Museveni of Uganda, 27 May 1997; lecture at the
Oxford Centre for Islamic Studies, 11 July 1997;
commemoration of the twentieth anniversary of Steve
Biko's death speech, East London, 12 September 1997;
Honorary Doctorate by Ben-Gurion University of the
Negev, Cape Town, speech, 19 September 1997;
Heritage Day speech, Robben Island, 24 September
1997; state banquet for Prime Minister Gujral of India,
Cape Town, 7 October 1997; Collar of the Nile
speech, Cairo, 21 October 1997; Colonel Gaddafi
speech, Tripoli, Libya, 22 October 1997; presentation
of the Africa Peace Award to Mozambique, Durban,
1 November 1997; state banquet for Prince Charles
speech, Cape Town, 4 November 1997; Foreign
Correspondents Association speech, Johannesburg,
21 November 1997; Freedom of the City of Cape
Town speech, 27 November 1997; Regina Mundi Day
speech, Soweto, 30 November 1997; Bram Fischer
Memorial Trust speech, Bloemfontein, 28 November
1997; International Day of Solidarity with the
Palestinian People speech, Pretoria, 4 December 1997;
report to the fiftieth National Conference of the ANC,
Mafikeng, 16 December 1997; farewell as President of
the ANC speech, Mafikeng, 20 December 1997; New
Year address, 31 December 1997